The Tongue Fast

The Tongue Fast

21 DAYS TO GLORIFYING SPEECH

Deborah Smith Pegues

Los Angeles

The Tongue Fast
21 Days to Glorifying Speech

Copyright © 2001 by Deborah Smith Pegues
Wisdom Publishing
P.O. Box 78201
Los Angeles, California 90016

Cover by Drawing Board Studios
(dbstudios171@cs.com)

Scripture quotations are from the King James Version of the Holy Bible (KJV), the New King James Version of the Holy Bible (NKJ), the New International Version of the Bible (NIV) and the New American Standard Bible (NAS).

Printed in the U.S.A.

CONTENTS

ACKNOWLEDGMENTS

I would like to thank Judge Mablean Ephriam who inspired the concept of a "tongue fast." My friend, Yvonne Gibson Johnson, insisted that I share it with others in the form of a book.

I also wish to express my sincere appreciation to my cheerleader, Redelia Fowler, for her enthusiasm, encouragement, and input.

Harold and Ruth Kelley once again unselfishly shared their mountain retreat and provided the ideal environment where I wrote significant sections of the book.

My husband, Darnell Pegues, graciously sacrificed our time together to give me space to write. Thank you, Sweetheart. There is none like you in all the earth.

PROLOGUE

Teachers often teach that which they need to learn themselves. I am no different. I am writing this book first and foremost for myself. I desire a wholesome tongue, one that always speaks what is pleasing to God. I have learned what James, the brother of Jesus, meant when he said, *"No man can tame the tongue . . ."* James 3:8. Neither New Year's resolutions, nor counting to ten nor any other human efforts will succeed. To "tame" means to bring from a state of unruliness to a state of submission. A person would have to live in total isolation to begin to accomplish such a feat with the tongue. And even then, his self-talk would probably be negative in some way and therefore rob him of a total victory in this area.

The only hope for the tongue is the Holy Spirit. The tongue must be bridled, brought into subjection by Him on a daily basis!

One of my spiritual mentors gave me a very simple tip for dealing with the negative propensities of the flesh. He said, "Whatever the flesh tells you to do, do the opposite." Well, that's a good place to start.

As you skimmed the list of the negative uses of the tongue in the table of contents, you may not have readily admitted that you are guilty of many of them. However, as you read this book with a desire to grow and to "own" behavior that you may have been denying, you will experience the freedom that only comes with embracing the truth. "*And ye shall know the truth, and the truth shall make you free*" John 8:32 (KJV).

Why a tongue fast? Why 21 days? Behaviorists have long concluded that it takes 21 days to develop a good habit or to break a bad one. In this book, I will challenge you to join me on a 21-day quest to become sensitive to the negative uses of the tongue and to "fast" or abstain from these verbal violations of godly principles.

Fasting (i.e., abstinence from food) is a spiritual discipline that few Christians embrace on a regular basis. After several incidents in which I realized that I showed little or no verbal wisdom, I knew that it was time to set aside a time of "tongue fasting" as a spiritual and practical means to breaking this stronghold. I found that a resolution, which emanated from my "flesh" or natural understanding, was not being effective against this unruly member. In the words of Jesus, *". . . this kind does not go out except by prayer and fasting"* Matthew 17:21 (NKJ).

Now I want to caution that this book is not designed to turn you into Passive Patsy who never expresses her boundaries, desires or dissatisfaction with a situation. Some things, though unpleasant or unpopular, must often be said. But I have learned that there is a *time* and a *way* to say everything. *"To every thing there is a season, and a time to every purpose under the heaven . . . a time to keep silence, and a time to speak . . ."* Ecclesiastes 3:1,7 (KJV).

We can rejoice knowing that we have already been empowered to use our tongues wisely. *"The Lord GOD hath given me the tongue of the learned, that I should know how to speak a word in season. . ."* Isaiah 50:4 (KJV). Surely we can discipline ourselves to speak the right words at the right time. Walking in spiritual maturity dictates that we speak in the right season, for the right reason and in the right tone. The challenge is to become aware of the negative uses of the tongue and then, through the power of the Holy Spirit to "do the opposite".

If you find that you are constantly at war with your tongue, I invite you to take up the challenge to stop your non-glorifying behavior. I guarantee you that at the end of this fast, you will be spiritually empowered and your tongue will begin to be a wellspring of life.

The Lying Tongue

The LORD detests lying lips,
but he delights in men who are truthful.
—Proverbs 12:22—

Truth must be at the base of all of our actions; lies make a shaky foundation. Lying comes in four primary forms: *deceitfulness, half-truths, exaggerations and flattery*.

Deceitfulness

Why do people lie? Obviously they fear the consequences of telling the truth. Therefore, they make a choice not to trust God to handle the situation. They lie to obtain money, to get a reduced price on a purchase, to hide immoral acts or to obtain other "benefits." Deceitfulness is a slap in God's face. It silently assumes Him to be a liar and one who will renege on His word. The deceiver feels that he must make his own way—by any means necessary. Deceitfulness is the most blatant form of lying.

Half-Truths

Joan Smith took the day off on Monday. She returned to work on Tuesday and explained to her boss that she had been absent because her elderly mother had been hospitalized. The truth of the matter is that Joan had only spent two hours at the hospital and six hours shopping! Joan's objective was to have her boss conclude that she had spent the entire day at her mother's bedside. She told her boss a half-truth.

I used to be the queen of half-truths. My rationale was that the portion of my statement actually verbalized was indeed true. I ignored the fact that the undisclosed information would have caused the hearer to draw a different conclusion. My husband finally impressed upon me the reality that any intent to deceive is a lie—period.

Exaggerating

Do you often embellish a story in order to get more attention from the listener? Exaggerating may seem harmless but it is another form of lying. The danger in exaggerating is that pretty soon you lose credibility with those who are familiar with your propensity to do so and they will began to discount everything you tell them. This is the paradox of exaggerating in that a person exaggerates to make something sound more credible but then loses his credibility because he exaggerates. I know several exaggeraters. Their friends jokingly say, "Now, Susie told me this story but you know you must discount at least half of what she tells you." What a terrible indictment against Susie's character. Do you think that this is how she would like to be remembered? Of course not!

Be sure that when you relate an incident or make an observation, stick to the facts at face value and resist the urge to be the center of attention by engaging in this form of lying.

Flattery

To flatter is to give someone an insincere compliment in order to gain his favor. Often the desired "favor" is not a material thing but "goodwill" and acceptance. The flatterer may have low self-worth and believes that others will like him if he compliments them.

Flattery reveals one's lack of faith in God's ability to give favor—despite the fact that we have been assured of it. "*For surely, O LORD, you bless the righteous; you surround them with your favor as with a shield*" Psalms 5:12 (NIV). God gave Esther favor and she was chosen queen of Persia; He gave Daniel favor and he and his three friends were allowed to select their own diet rather than eat the non-Kosher food of their captors. In neither case was flattery necessary.

Can you think of a time that you flattered someone? How did you feel afterwards? Unless you have grown used to such behavior and have become totally insensitive to the Holy Spirit, flattering someone will probably cause you to feel that you have violated your integrity. Perhaps you haven't heard of God's plans for the flatterer. *"The LORD shall cut off all flattering lips, and the tongue that speaketh proud things"* Psalms 12:3 (KJV).

Is flattery really worth being cut off from the blessings of God?

The eternal destiny of the liar has been sealed by God: *". . . and all liars shall have their part in the lake which burns with fire and brimstone, which is the second death"* Revelations 21:8 (NKJ). Death means separation. The first death is the separation of the spirit from the body; the second death is eternal separation of the spirit from God. Eternal separation is too expensive a price to pay for deceitfulness. The psalmist knew the consequences of deceitfulness and constantly implored God to keep him out of this pit. Consider his plea. *"Deliver my soul, O LORD, from lying lips, and from a deceitful tongue"* Psalms 120:2 (KJV).

Have you been trusting God or do you need to join the psalmist in his prayer for deliverance?

Personalized Scriptural Affirmation

"My mouth speaks what is true, for my lips detest wickedness. All the words of my mouth are just; none of them is crooked or perverse."
—PROVERBS 8:7-8 (NIV)

DAY 2

The Hasty Tongue

Do you see a man hasty in his words?
There is more hope for a fool than for him.
—Proverbs 29:20 (NKJ)—

Do you sometimes offend others because you don't engage your brain before shifting your tongue into drive? The communication of the hasty tongue is done too quickly to be wise or accurate. I am totally convinced that no matter how holy you are, you will eventually offend somebody because of hasty speech. *"For in many things we offend all. If any man offend not in word, the same is a **perfect** man, and able also to bridle the* *whole body"* James 3:2 (KJV). Since no one has reached perfection and since we can never be totally aware of all of the sensitivities of others, we can only ask the Holy Spirit to help us. I have seen Christians innocently offend others in an attempt to interject humor into a situation. What is so amazing is how overly sensitive many Christians are! I try to practice not being so easily offended and often give others the benefit of the doubt when they make a hasty remark.

Seeing that I was challenged by a hasty tongue, one of my mentors admonished me, "Stop, think and pray before you speak." James said it best. "*Wherefore, my beloved brethren, let every man be swift to hear, slow to speak . . .*" James 1:19 (KJV). Have you ever wondered why God gave us two ears and one mouth? A good pause will serve you well in the long run.

Personalized Scriptural Affirmation

"I am swift to hear and slow to speak. The Lord has set a guard over my mouth and He keeps watch over the door of my lips."
—(JAMES 1:19; PSALMS 141:3)

DAY 3

The Divisive Tongue

*These six things doth the LORD hate: yea, seven are an abomination unto him: A proud look, a lying tongue, and hands that shed innocent blood, An heart that deviseth wicked imaginations, feet that be swift in running to mischief, A false witness that speaketh lies, **and he that soweth discord among brethren.***
—PROVERBS 6:16-19 (KJV)—

Did you know that God hates strife and division? Have you allowed your tongue to be an instrument of divisiveness? Anytime that you tell another person something negative that someone else has said about him, you must realize that your actions could be divisive. This is not to say that you should not warn someone about another person who is not acting in his best interest. Just be honest about your underlying motive. You may be trying to gain favor or to indirectly communicate your own feelings about the person at the expense of another. Whatever the rationale, the end result is still the same—and God is not pleased with divisiveness.

God commands His blessing at the place of unity (Psalm 133). Satan knows the power that we have when we work in harmony with each other. That is why he tries on every hand to bring division. He only knows two forms of math: subtraction and division. Our Heavenly Father, on the other hand, adds and multiplies; He only takes away our sins.

When was the last time that you caused a conflict by using a divisive tongue? Why did you do it? How did you feel afterwards? When was the last time that you had an opportunity to reconcile two parties in conflict and did so? You must make it your business, as a Christian, to be a peacemaker. Understand that peacemaker actively seeks to make peace and to bridge the gap in divided relationships.

Personalized Scriptural Affirmation

"I am blessed for I am a peacemaker and I shall be called a child of God."
—MATTHEW 5:9 (KJV)

DAY 4

The Boasting Tongue

*"Let another praise you, and not your own mouth;
someone else, and not your own lips."*
—PROVERBS 27:2 (NIV)—

Are you so proud of your accomplishments
or your possessions that you cannot help but
boast about them? King Solomon, who was
wisdom personified, cautioned us to avoid
boasting. Boasting implies that your good
fortune is a result of your own efforts. Have
you forgotten that everything that you have
came from God? King Nebuchadnezzar did.
One day, as he was strolling on the roof of

his palace, he boasted to himself, *"Is not this the great Babylon I have built as the royal residence, by my mighty power and for the glory of my majesty?"*

Scripture tells us that God interrupted his proud moment and declared to him that his kingdom had been taken from him effectively immediately! He was driven from the palace and forced to live as a common derelict. His hair grew like the feathers of an eagle and his nails like the claws of a bird. He even became mentally challenged. It was not until he acknowledged God as the ruler over all that his sanity returned and his kingdom was restored. Hear his testimony:

> *"At the end of that time, I, Nebuchadnezzar, raised my eyes toward heaven, and my sanity was restored. Then I praised the Most High; I honored and glorified Him who lives forever. His dominion is an eternal dominion; His kingdom endures from generation to generation. All the peoples of the earth are regarded as nothing. He does as He pleases with the powers of heaven and*

> *the peoples of the earth. No one can hold*
> *back His hand or say to Him: 'What have*
> *you done?'"*
> —DANIEL 4:34-35 (NIV)

Just as the drum major goes before the band in a parade, pride goes before a fall. We must learn to consciously take the back seat when pride screams for the front row. Study the fate of proud men in the bible. Meditate on scriptures that deal with humility and pride. I have framed the passage below and keep it in my view in my office.

> *For who makes you different from anyone*
> *else? What do you have that you did not*
> *receive? And if you did receive it, why do*
> *you boast as though you did not?*
> —1 CORINTHIANS 4:7 (NIV)

Whatever skills or talents God has given to you, they are for His glory. If your popularity increases, don't be intoxicated by the accolades. Remember that praise is like perfume, if you consume it, it will kill you!

Personalized Scriptural Affirmation

"But by the grace of God, I am what I am. . ."
—1 CORINTHIANS 15:10 (NIV)

DAY 5

The Self-Deprecating Tongue

Moses said to the LORD, "O Lord, I have never been eloquent, neither in the past nor since you have spoken to your servant.
I am slow of speech and tongue."
—EXODUS 4:10 (NIV)—

You engage in self-deprecation when you think or speak of yourself as being of little or no worth and thereby minimize the value of what you "bring to the table" or have to offer. Notice how Satan seeks to take us from one extreme to the other? He either tries to make us boastful or bashful. He tries to make us think that we are "da bomb" (slang for "really hot stuff", "all that") or "done bombed" (totally blew it!). Don't be ignorant of his tricks.

Self-deprecation is often disguised as humility; but in reality it is a rejection of the word of God that assures us that we can do all things through Christ who strengthens or empowers us. Watch those negative labels that you put on yourself. What others call you is not important. It is only what you call yourself that matters.

Consider the account of Jesus and the man who had been possessed by demons for a long time. *Jesus asked him, "What is thy name?" And he said, "Legion" because many devils were entered into him* Luke 8:30 (KJV). A "legion" was a major unit of the Roman army consisting of up to 6000 troops; "Legion" was not this man's given name. Being possessed by a legion of demons was a state of being that he had come to "own" or accept as a permanent reality. He had dealt with the problem for so long that he defined himself by his experience.

Have you had an experience that you have allowed to define you? Perhaps you have labeled yourself "Fatso" because you have battled your weight a long time with no victory in sight. Have you defined yourself as "Victim" because you were truly victimized more than once? Or, "Failure" because you are divorced? How have you defined yourself? Abandon the negative labels! Call yourself "Victorious".

Self-deprecation displeases God. When Moses complained that he was inadequate to lead the Israelites out of Egypt because of his speech impediment, God became upset:

> *The LORD said to him, "Who gave man his mouth? Who makes him deaf or mute? Who gives him sight or makes him blind? Is it not I, the LORD? Now go; I will help you speak and will teach you what to say."*
> —EXODUS 4: 11-12 (NIV)

Reject that spirit of inadequacy. Without God you can do nothing anyway; but with Him you can do all things. Because of the reality of this word, you can walk in confidence—not in self—but in the grace of God that empowers you.

Personalized Scriptural Affirmation

*"And God is able to make **all** grace abound toward me; so that I **always** having **all** sufficiency in **all** things, may abound to **every** good work."*
—2 Corinthians 9:8 (KJV)

DAY 6

The Slandering Tongue

"Whoever secretly slanders his neighbor,
him I will destroy. . . ."
—PSALMS 101:5 (NKJ)—

To slander is to make a malicious, false or even true statement about another with the intent of damaging his reputation, character or good name. The slanderer communicates his information out of a heart of hatred or envy. Slandering, backbiting and defaming are all shades of the same evil. There won't be any slanderers in heaven.

> *"LORD, who may dwell in your sanctu-*
> *ary? Who may live on your holy hill? He*
> *whose walk is blameless and who does what*
> *is righteous, who speaks the truth from his*
> *heart and has no **slander** on his tongue,*
> *who does his neighbor no wrong and casts*
> *no slur on his fellowman."*
>
> —PSALMS 15:1-3

Can you recall a time that you communi-
cated slanderous information about someone? What was you motive in doing so? Why
did you feel the need to diminish that
person's character in the eyes of another?
Were you speaking out of the pain of being
hurt by her? Did you envy her accomplishments? Have you not learned how to let
your envy motivate you rather than cause
you to defame another?

Have you ever been slandered? How did
you respond? Consider the Apostle Paul's
wise counsel on responding to this malicious
act:

> *"We work hard with our own hands.*
> *When we are cursed, we bless; when we are*

*persecuted, we endure it; when we are
slandered, we answer kindly. . . ."*
—(1 CORINTHIANS 4:12–13 (NIV)

Personalized Scriptural Affirmation

*"I refuse to be a slanderer. Philippians 4:8 is my
conversation sifter, consequently whatever things
are true, noble, just, pure, lovely, and of good
report, if there is any virtue and if there is
anything praiseworthy about someone, I comment
only on these things. Further, when I am
slandered, I will answer kindly. I will not
retaliate since vengeance belongs to God."*

DAY 7

The Gossiping Tongue

The words of a gossip are like choice morsels;
they go down to a man's inmost parts.
—PROVERBS 18:8 (NIV)—

Gossip is idle, often malicious talk about the personal affairs of another. And, yes, it can be as delectable as a "choice morsel"—especially to those who don't have a life! Now, I'm certain that everyone reading this book has been guilty of partaking of this popular pastime-either as a bearer or a hearer. Did you know that gossiping could lower your sense of self-worth? How? When you gossip, you tend to realize that you are not walking in integrity. We feel best about ourselves when we do things that are pleasing to God; we were created for His pleasure.

So what's the solution? How do you stop gossiping? Catch yourself before you indulge! Ask yourself why you are being a bearer. Do you need to be the center of attention or to feel empowered by knowing something about somebody that the hearer doesn't know? Are you envious of that person's accomplishments? And why are you willing to use the temple of God as a "trash receptacle" by being a receiver of gossip? Are you bored with your life and need more meaningful activities? It has been my observation that those who are ardently pursuing their own goals and aspirations are less likely to spend time obsessing with the affairs of another.

Heed the advice of Apostle Peter: *"But let none of you suffer as a murderer, a thief, an evildoer, or as a busybody in other people's matters"* 1 Peter 4:15 (NKJ). Start an all out campaign against gossip. Let everyone know that you will not be a bearer or a hearer of "choice morsels" about anyone. Declare your environment, whether at work, at home or at play to be a "gossip-free zone". When people come into my office and start ungodly talk, I point to my tongue and exclaim, "Tongue Fast!" They immediately know that their conversation will not be indulged. Now, refusing to engage in gossip may cost you an acquaintance or two; but hang in there. God will supply your need for friends. And, yes, you will experience a rise in your self-esteem when you, with complete dependence on the Father can humbly declare, *"The words of my mouth and the meditation of my heart are acceptable in thy sight, O LORD, my strength and my redeemer"* Psalms 19:14 (KJV).

Personalized Scriptural Affirmation

"I am not a busybody in other people's matters. Therefore, I do no yield my tongue as an instrument of gossip."

The Betraying Tongue

*A gossip betrays a confidence,
but a trustworthy man keeps a secret.*
—PROVERBS 11:13 (NIV)—

Betrayal is a more egregious or blatant act than gossip. A gossip may not necessarily harbor any ill will toward his victim, however, a betrayer divulges information in breach of a confidence. He gives information to the "enemy" and commits relational treason by violating the trust someone has placed in him. This ungodly use of the tongue is designed to hurt or disadvantage. Judas was able to be-

tray Jesus with very little effort because he
was familiar with His comings and goings.

> *Now Judas, who betrayed him, **knew the
> place**, because Jesus had often met there
> with his disciples.*
>
> —JOHN 18:2 (NIV)

Judas used his inside knowledge of Jesus'
habits to hurt him. Later, his betrayal caused
him such self-loathing that he committed
suicide. Such an act must surely eat away at
one's self-esteem and sense of dignity. Have
you ever betrayed someone's confidence? Be
honest. Why did you do it? What was your
payoff? Did you gain some advantage because of it? Were you feeling envious at the
time? Was there an unresolved conflict be-
tween the two of you? Have you repented
for this sin?

On the other hand, has someone betrayed
your confidence? Were you reaping what you
had sown? What valuable lesson did you learn
from the incident? Have you released the of-
fender in your heart and desire no vengeance? If not, you are still bound to him and

he is still controlling your life. Let it go, God saw the betrayal *before* it happened and *while* it was happening. Since He chose not to intervene, accept it as part of His sovereign plan for your life. Learn from the burn, but forgive to live. Remind yourself that in the final analysis, the incident will work together for your good because you love God and are called according to His purpose.

Decide today to strive to be a totally trustworthy person, one that others can depend upon to guard their secrets. Ask God to send you such a person also. If you already have a trustworthy friend, thank God for blessing you with such a rare jewel.

Personalized Scriptural Affirmation

"I am a trustworthy person and never betray a confidence."

The Belittling Tongue

*Do not let any unwholesome talk come out of your mouths, but only what is helpful for **building others up** according to their needs, that it may benefit those who listen.*
—EPHESIANS 4:29 (NIV)—

Do people feel better about themselves after spending time with you? Or, are your expectations so high that you focus on their shortcomings rather than their assets? If someone speaks well of a person that you envy, do you follow up with a disparaging remark? Are you so insecure that you can only feel good about yourself by denigrating others?

> *"Therefore encourage one another, and build up one another, just as you also are doing."*
>
> —1 THESSALONIANS 5:11 (NAS)

We recently had a room expanded at our home. It was interesting to watch how the hammer was used in the demolition as well as the construction process. Words are like that; they can tear down or they can build. How do you use your words mostly?

During your tongue fast, act as if you are a coach to your family members, employees, co-workers and others in your sphere of influence. Now, I know from experience that if you tend to be one of those hard-driving goal-oriented people, coaching may be a challenge initially. Perhaps you are from that school of thought that believes an employee's paycheck is encouragement enough—especially if he is more than adequately compensated. Beware! Thou art stuck in the stone ages and in dire need of a mind-set change. If you want to maximize productivity, then learn how to build up your employees. I have found that it is not my *natural inclination* to want to coach poor performers; I just want them out. In with the new superstars! What I have learned is that a little positive affirmation; some handholding and lots of communication will often yield the productivity and the loyalty that may not accompany the cocky superstar.

Make it a habit to affirm your family members and friends. Tell your wife that she is the only woman for you; express your appreciation for your husband's sense of responsibility; applaud your teenager for avoiding drugs and alcohol; thank a friend for keeping your secrets! Resist the temptation to constantly "fix" something about them. Accept them as they are and remember that you only have them for a season.

Personalized Scriptural Affirmation

"No unwholesome talk comes out of my mouths but only what is helpful for building others up according to their needs, that it may benefit those who listen."

DAY 10

The Cynical Tongue

*Blessed is the man that walketh not in the counsel
of the ungodly, nor standeth in the way of sinners,
nor sitteth in the seat of the **scornful**.*
—PSALMS 1:1 (KJV)—

One who is cynical is scornful of the motives,
virtue or integrity of others. Such was Eliab,
David's oldest brother. When David went
down to the scene of the battle and saw
Goliath, the Philistine giant intimidating the Israelites, he became indignant. He emphatically
and confidently stated that he could take care of
this "uncircumcised Philistine". Circumcision
(the cutting away of the male foreskin) was a
sign of God's covenant of protection and provi-

sion for the Israelites. David knew that this bully had no such covenant with God; only the Israelites could claim such a benefit. David was particularly secure in the covenant.

> Now Eliab, his oldest brother, heard when he spoke to the men; and Eliab's anger burned against David and he said, "Why have you come down? And with whom have you left those few sheep in the wilderness? I know your insolence and the wickedness of your heart; for you have come down in order to see the battle. But David said, "What have I done now? Was it not just a question?"
> —1 SAMUEL 17:28-29 (NAS)

Eliab, whose name meant, "God is my father" (imagine one with such a name running from the giant), scorned David's confidence and his motives. He was cynical.

Cynicism is like venom; it poisons the atmosphere wherever it is present. Resorting to it will also poison your spirit and that of others. Find one cynical employee, parishioner or family member and pretty soon those with weaker minds are chiming in and perpetuating the negative conversation.

As you proceed on your tongue fast, really begin to observe your comments in various settings and determine if you are being cynical or scornful. If so, you are hindering your blessings. Retire from cynicism today.

Personalized Scriptural Affirmation

"I am blessed because I walk not in the counsel of the ungodly, nor standeth in the way of sinners, nor sitteth in the seat of the scornful."

DAY 11

The "Know-It-All" Tongue

~∞∞∞∞~

A prudent man conceals knowledge,
but the heart of fools proclaims folly.
—PROVERBS 12: 23 (NAS)—

Are you so all-knowing that you cannot refrain from giving unsolicited advice? Do you have an unusually high regard for your opinion? Do you regularly use the expression, "You should . . . ?" Please allow me to gently remind you that most emotionally healthy people usually resent someone who always assumes that he or she knows what's best for them.

Give people the benefit of the doubt. Even if you feel that you have earned the right to speak into someone's life, proceed with caution. "Have you considered . . . ?" sounds a lot less controlling and will be more welcomed (especially by men) than "You should . . . ." Married women, take heed! Real men aren't looking for Mother. Right before I got married, one of my spiritual mentors gave me a bit of advice. "We know that you're smart," she cautioned, "but don't know everything. Let your husband know some things sometimes." I have heeded this simple wisdom for over 22 years with good results.

Even if you have knowledge and insight into a certain situation, sometimes it's prudent to keep silent and give another the joy and fulfillment of explaining it to you. Letting someone share info with you that you already know—without letting him know that you know it—can be great training in humility and emotional maturity.

Personalized Scriptural Affirmation

"I am prudent and therefore I practice concealing my knowledge."

The Harsh Tongue

She openeth her mouth with wisdom;
*and in her tongue is the **law** of kindness.*
—PROVERBS 31:26 (KJV)—

In my impatience and frustration with in-
competence or low productivity in others, I
have often made harsh remarks. When I
have worked in a company culture where fir-
ings for poor work were rare, I felt that a
tongue-lashing was my only recourse. The
end result has never been positive.

The wise woman of Proverbs 31 made it
a law—a rule of conduct—to speak kindly to
others. There is never any justification for

being unkind. Christ was never so. If you claim to have the mind of Christ, you won't *practice* such behavior either.

Kind words are warm-hearted, understanding and sympathetic. As a good steward of the grace of God, you must extend that grace to others. Speak a kind word today to someone, especially someone who may not deserve it—isn't that what grace is all about?

Caution! This does not mean that you are to bury your head in the sand and not deal with a problematic situation. However, you must get God's words for they do not return void.

> *"So shall my word be that goeth forth out of my mouth: it shall not return unto me void, but it shall accomplish that which I please, and it shall prosper in the thing whereto I sent it."*
>
> —(ISAIAH 55:11 (KJV)

If you are a verbal abuser, ask God for deliverance today. *He who is slow to anger is better than the mighty, and he who rules his spirit than he who takes a city"* Proverbs 16:32

(NKJ). Begin to take control over that destructive behavior by the power of the Holy Spirit. Remember that cutting words never die and cannot be recovered. Don't let verbal abuse be named among your character traits.

Personalized Scriptural Affirmation

" I open my mouth with wisdom. The law of kindness is in my tongue."

DAY 13

The Judgmental Tongue

*"Do not judge, or you too will be judged.
For in the same way you judge others,
you will be judged. . ."*
—MATTHEW 7:1–2 (NIV)—

The judgmental person engages in a critical, faultfinding assessment of another person's behavior based upon certain prejudices. Isn't it amazing that we judge others by their *actions* but judge ourselves by our *intentions?"* Jesus was emphatic about his displeasure with judgmental folks.

> *"Why do you look at the speck of sawdust in your brother's eye and pay no attention to the plank in your own eye? How can you say to your brother, 'Let me take the speck out of your eye,' when all the time there is a plank in your own eye? You hypocrite, first take the plank out of your own eye, and then you will see clearly to remove the speck from your brother's eye."*
>
> —MATTHEW 7:3–5 (NIV)

The Pharisees must have been a miserable bunch. They were always looking for something to nit-pick about—even in dealing with Jesus. Consider Jesus' response to them:

> *"You judge by human standards; I pass judgment on no one. But if I do judge, my decisions are right, because I am not alone. I stand with the Father, who sent me."*
>
> —JOHN 8:15–16 (NIV)

Jesus based his judgment of people's behavior on nothing other than God's standard. We must learn to focus more on judging ourselves than "mote hunting" in the matters of others. Pray for those whom you observe walking contrary to God's standards—but abandon the criticism.

Personalized Scriptural Affirmation

"I do not judge others or I too will be judged. For in the same way that I judge, I will be judged . . . ."

DAY 14

The Self-Absorbed Tongue

*"Each of you should look not only
to your own interests,
but also to the interests of others."*
—PHILIPPIANS 2:4 (NIV)—

Are most of your conversations with others centered on you and your issues? A self-absorbed tongue will surely alienate others as almost everyone desires or indeed needs to be the focus of attention occasionally.

Haman, the Persian government official in the book of Esther was self-absorption personified. On and on he went about himself!

> *"Haman boasted to them about **his** vast wealth, **his** many sons, and all the ways the king had honored **him** and how he had elevated **him** above the other nobles and officials."*
>
> —ESTHER 5:11 (NIV)

Become conscious of this character flaw in your own life and ask God to make you genuinely interested in others. My friend, Frank Wilson, who wrote numerous gold releases for Motown Records before devoting his life to God, is such a person. He can talk to someone for an extended period of time and maintain a genuine interest in him. Everyone loves being in his presence!

If you find yourself cornered by a self-absorbed person, try asking him to give you some advice or input about an issue that does not involve him. If the culprit is a close friend, gently tell her, "I really need you to listen to me right now."

If you happen to be the self-absorbed one, challenge yourself to go a whole day or more without making your issues the focus of your conversations.

Personalized Scriptural Affirmation

"I look not only to my own interests, but to the interest of others. Therefore, my issues are not the primary topic of my conversations."

DAY 15

The "Cussing" Tongue
❦

*"Out of the same mouth proceed
blessing and cursing.
My brethren, these things ought not to be so."*
—JAMES 3: 8–10 (NKJ)—

Using profane and obscene language is un-
becoming to a child of God. Yet, many so-
called Christians use four letter words as
freely as they drink water. Why?

*"But no man can tame the tongue. It is
an unruly evil, full of deadly poison. With
it we bless our God and Father, and with
it we curse men, who have been made in
the similitude of God."*
—JAMES 3: 8–10 (NKJ)

I know a Christian woman who goes on extended fasts and yet regularly uses "hell" and "damn" as expletives. When a co-worker confronted her about her use of such non-glorifying expressions, she said, "These words are in the Bible." I have heard other Christians snicker about her hypocrisy behind her back. She and they need to go on a tongue fast! I believe that a person who uses profanity often lacks an adequate vocabulary to express himself and therefore feels that he must "cuss" for his words to have impact. If you are challenged in this area, start to develop a communication style that is direct and clear—and without hostility. You will find that expletives are completely unnecessary.

Most of all stay on an extended "Tongue Fast" and daily ask God to purify your tongue. Declare your freedom from the bondage of profane language.

Personalized Scriptural Affirmation

"Cursing does not proceed out of my mouth. Today I give God full charge of my tongue. By His grace I will only speak words that will bring honor to His name."

The Complaining Tongue

I cry aloud with my voice to the LORD;
I make supplication with my voice to the LORD.
I pour out my complaint before Him;
I declare my trouble before Him.
—PSALMS 142:1–2 (NAS)—

Complaining can only be effective if you complain to the one who can change your situation. Otherwise, it is an exercise in futility, a useless consumption of time. The psalmist did not bore, frustrate or waste the time of others with his complaints. He took his issues to the Lord, the one who could effect change. Such was also the approach of the five daughters of Zelophehad (Numbers 27) who, because they were women, were prohibited by law from receiving an inheritance in the Promised Land. Their father had died in the wilderness and had no sons to inherit his portion of the land. Consequently, his daughters, not having a father, brother, husband, son or any other man in their immediate family were left out in the cold. Rather than complaining to others, they called a "congressional hearing" and presented their petition for an inheritance to Moses and the leaders. When Moses took their problem to God, He agreed with the daughters and granted their request. What do you think the outcome would have been had they simply complained to anyone in the multitude who would listen rather than those in authority?

During your tongue fast, become aware of how often you complain. Resist the constant "ain't it awful" party. Trust me, others will be glad that you did and will stop dreading conversations with you. This is not to say that you should not seek an occasional sympathetic ear or wise counsel from a valued source. However, if you are going to ignore their advice and continue to rehearse the problem each time that you converse, beware. Thy listener shall soon become weary of thee! When you feel a complaint coming on, replace it with a statement of gratitude or a declaration of a scripture that you have personalized.

Personalized Scriptural Affirmation:

"All things are working together for my good, because I love God and I am called according to His purpose. Therefore, I will not complain. In the name of Jesus, I come against any and all satanic involvement in my circumstances. I accept God's sovereign plan for my life."

The Retaliating Tongue

*"Do not repay evil with evil or **insult with insult**,
but with blessing, because to this you were called
so that you may inherit a blessing."*
—*1 PETER 3:9 (NIV)—*

The thrill of a verbal retaliation is only a
fleeting pleasure for those who love God
and His word; the remorse and conviction
for succumbing to such a sin tend to linger.

Retaliation used to be one of my biggest
challenges. That's why I praise God for His
Holy Spirit who convicts, guides and works
in me to do His good pleasure. It feels great
to respond God's way. Sure, Satan will taunt
you and call you a wimp. But your reward

will be a higher place in God. I am amazed at how much I have grown in this area. I know from many experiences that "*A soft answer turneth away wrath: but grievous words stir up anger*" Proverbs 15:1 (KJV).

My breakthrough in this area came when I began studying conflict management. I learned that the root meaning of the word "retaliation" is to "return the punishment"; thus, to retaliate is to avenge a wrong. Vengeance is God's job; not mine.

> *Beloved, do not avenge yourselves, but rather give place to wrath; for it is written, "Vengeance is Mine, I will repay," says the Lord.*
>
> —ROMANS 12:19 (NKJ)

I can not tell you that I bat a 1000 in this area in every situation, but whenever I do strike out, it's because I have ignored the prompting of the Holy Spirit and made a conscious decision to take God's job; to succumb to the desire of the my flesh.

Decide now that your very next conflict will find you responding with a "soft answer". Just try it! Feel yourself grow ten feet tall in the spirit.

Personalized Scriptural Affirmation

"I will not repay evil with evil or insult with insult, but with blessing, because to this I have been called so that I may inherit a blessing."
—1 PETER 3:9

DAY 18

The Accusing Tongue

". . . for the accuser of our brethren has been thrown down, who accuses them before our God day and night."
—Revelation 12:10 (NAS)—

Have you ever been falsely accused? Have your motives been called into question when you knew that they were pure? Have you ever charged someone with wrongdoing before you established evidence of his or her guilt? When you do so, you emulate the behavior of Satan, the official accuser of God's children. False accusations hurt.

Emotional and spiritual maturity dictate that you seek first to understand rather than making an accusation. Look at the example that God set in the Garden of Eden when Adam and Eve blew it. He could have easily said, "Adam, you sinner, I should never have trusted you in my garden!" God's non-accusatory style in confronting Adam and Eve about their trespass provides a powerful model for those of us who tend to accuse before getting an understanding.

> *Then the LORD God called to Adam and said to him, "Where are you?" So he said, "I heard your voice in the garden, and I was afraid because I was naked; and I hid myself." And He said, "Who told you that you were naked? Have you eaten from the tree of which I commanded you that you should not eat?"*
>
> —GENESIS 3:9–11 (NKJ)

Asking a clarifying question and listening to the response are the key steps in overcoming an accusing tongue. I repeat, ask and listen.

Personalized Scriptural Affirmation

"The Lord GOD has given me the tongue of the learned, that I should know how to speak a word in season to him who is weary. He awakens me morning by morning; He awakens my ear to hear as the learned."
—ISAIAH 50:4 (NKJ)

DAY *19*

The Discouraging Tongue

"They helped every one his neighbour; and every one said to his brother, 'Be of good courage.'"
—Isaiah 41:6 (KJV)—

Has anyone ever dampened your hope, confidence or enthusiasm by raising objections to your proposed action? The discourager's motive may not have been impure, but rather a reflection of his own lack of faith in God's ability to "*. . . do exceeding abundantly beyond all that we ask or think, according to the power that works within us*" Ephesians 3:20 (NAS).

Are you a discourager? Can you listen to the dreams and plans of another without making disheartening remarks? This is not to say that you shouldn't offer objective input. However, a well-phrased questions can be much more effective than a straight out "That's impossible!" For example, "How did you determine the market for your product?" sounds better than "Gee, I don't think that many people would be interested in that!"

Moses reprimanded certain Israelites for their discouragement and lack of support of their brothers.

> *But Moses said to the sons of Gad and to the sons of Reuben, "Shall your brothers go to war while you yourselves sit here? Now why are you **discouraging** the sons of Israel from crossing over into the land which the LORD has given them?"*
> —NUMBERS 32:6–7 (NAS)

Even if you cannot catch the vision of another, at least agree to stand in faith with the person for God's perfect will for the proposed endeavor. Do not allow your tongue to be a tool of discouragement.

Personalized Scriptural Affirmation:

"I always exhort everyone to be of good courage."

The Loquacious Tongue

*When words are many, sin is not absent,
but he who holds his tongue is wise.*
—PROVERBS 10:19 (NIV)

Have you ever talked to someone who seemed to have diarrhea of the mouth? On and on she goes—from one topic to another. Well, know from henceforth that the proper word for this malady is *loquaciousness (pronounced: low-kway-shus-ness) and* is just a big word for a "motor mouth". While it is generally concluded that females have cornered the market on this use of the tongue, men can be guilty too. Now, I admit that I am not a "silent lamb" by any stretch of the imagination. In fact my husband says that I will talk to a stop sign (I represent that!). However, I take great pleasure in listening to others. In fact, people who are reputed to be shy, talk to me freely.

When I am in the presence of an incessant talker, I often wonder if that person is lonely, has few opportunities to talk to others or just plain loves the sound of her voice. Whatever the motivation, excessive talking tends not to glorify God. I heard someone say that any conversation that lasts more than ten minutes will usually end up on the wrong path. The Apostle Paul admonished the Thessalonians to " . . . study to be quiet . . ." 1Thessalonians 4:11. To "study" implies a striving or intense effort. It will take some work to overcome this entrenched habit.

If you often find your conversation veering down the path of sin because of your loquaciousness, try these quick detours:

- Simply stop talking and ask the other person an open-ended question that would cause him to respond with more than a simple "Yes" or "No". For example, "John, what do you think about . . . ?"

- Make the talking count. My mentor, the late Dr. Juanita Smith, would often say, "I am not a woman of few words, but I love to talk about the things of God." Share an interesting news story that you've heard or share an insight that God has given you on a scripture. For example, rather than succumbing to a negative conversation, I keep telling everyone about my "Tongue Fast" and the truths that God has revealed from His word during my search of the scriptures. They listen with great interest and benefit.

Personalized Scriptural Affirmation:

"When my words are many, sin is not absent, but when I hold my tongue, I am considered wise."

The Indiscreet Tongue

*Discretion will protect you,
and understanding will guard you.*
—PROVERBS 2:11 (NIV)—

After the great flood that destroyed most of the earth, Noah planted a vineyard. One day, he got carried away and drank too much of the wine. His son, Ham, discovered him in his tent—drunk and naked. Scripture tells us that Ham ". . . *saw his father's nakedness and told his two brothers outside*" Gen. 9:22. Exercising more discretion than Ham, his brothers would not even look on their father, but backed into the tent and covered him with a garment. Their discretion was a sign of their maturity. One who is discreet shows prudence and wise self-restraint in speech and behavior—and always reaps a positive consequence.

The price of indiscretion can be costly. Some subject matter should simply be off limits for discussion. You would be wise to never discuss your salary or bonus—especially with other company personnel. Your sex life should also be off limits as an item of discussion with a non-counseling outsider.

Ham's indiscretion proved costly for him. When Noah sobered up, he realized his shame and was sorely displeased with the indiscreet manner in which Ham had handled the situation. Noah cursed him and doomed his descendents to slavery.

Have you ever found out something about a leader or other prominent person and could not refrain from telling someone? If God has trusted you enough to reveal someone's nakedness (sin), have you ever considered that you were not to "see" and "tell" but rather to cover that nakedness with discretion and intercession?

Having grown up in church, I have seen the nakedness of many leaders. God has often reminded me that He was trusting me, not to "cover up", but to "cover with". It can be a very uncomfortable position. God may even call you to confront the individual regarding his or her nakedness. He did so with Nathan the prophet who confronted David about his adultery with Bathsheba and his subsequent murder of her husband to cover it up (II Samuel 12). Whatever God mandates, do it His way. A public revelation is not always necessary as it can cause irreparable damage to the body of Christ. David's sin with Bathsheba never became the topic of a public scandal. However, David suffered the consequences through his family and other areas of his life. A leader's punishment is God's business.

Caution! If you serve in a position of authority, such as a member of a Board of Directors, then you are obligated to deal with ungodly behavior in a leader. Confront with love and compassion. No one is perfect and no one has 20–20 vision on himself. Remember that. God may someday show someone your nakedness. Pray that it will be handled with wisdom. Plant the seed of discretion now!

Personalized Scriptural Affirmation:

"My discretion will protect me and understanding will guard me."

Epilogue

Okay. So you have finished reading this book and it probably did not take 21 days to do so. The reading was just step one; now, you are ready to hone in on your particular areas of challenge. You may have to spend 10 days on the "Lying Tongue" and no time on the "Cussing Tongue". You may even decide to "tongue fast" one day each week rather than 21 days straight. I guarantee you, however, that as you meditate on each scripture that speaks to the ungodly uses of the tongue discussed herein, you will become highly sensitive to the areas where you need extra grace and deliverance.

To assess your progress, review the Negative Tongue Assessment Checklist at Appendix A on a regular basis. The checklist summarizes the twenty-one negative uses of the tongue that we have discussed.

When you can answer "No" to every question on a daily basis, you can rest assured that the Holy Spirit has gotten the upper hand on that little unruly member that no man can tame. You are now ready to turn your focus away from the negative uses of the tongue and begin to deliberately target some positive uses. You will now major in building, dispersing wisdom, exhorting, inspiring faith and giving life to your hearers. To stay on this positive path, regularly meditate on the scriptures in Appendix B: The Path to Positive Proclamations. These scriptures will fortify your inner man and revolutionize your conversations. Continue to decree that the words of your mouth have become acceptable in the sight of the Lord, your strength and your redeemer. Finally, act as if every word that you speak will become your personal reality!

Appendix A

The Negative Tongue Assessment
Checklist

To measure your progress, ask yourself the following questions at the end of each day. On a separate sheet, note the number of "Yes's".

___Did I engage in any form of lying?
___Did I speak too hastily?
___Were my words divisive?
___Did I boast?
___Did I engage in self-deprecation?
___Did I slander or backbite?
___Did I gossip?
___Did I betray someone's trust?
___Did I belittle someone?
___Was I cynical, scornful or sarcastic?
___Did I speak as a "Know-It-All"?
___Did I use harsh or abusive words?
___Was I critical or judgmental?

____Was I self-absorbed in my
    conversations?
____Did I use profanity?
____Did I complain?
____Did I retaliate?
____Did I accuse someone?
____Was I discouraging?
____Did I simply talk too much?
____Was I indiscreet in my discussions?

If you answered "No" to all of the questions above, rejoice—but do not relax. Quietly ask the Holy Spirit to show you your next focus area of spiritual development. Know that you will reach perfection only when you get to heaven.

Appendix B

The Path to Positive Proclamations

I will bless the LORD at all times.
His praise shall continually be in my mouth.
—PSALMS 34:1 (KJV)—

Let your speech be always with grace,
seasoned with salt,
that ye may know how ye ought
to answer every man.
—COLOSSIANS 4:6 (KJV)—

Do all things without complaining and disputing.
—PHILIPPIANS 2:14 (NKJ)—

Listen, for I have worthy things to say;
I open my lips to speak what is right.
My mouth speaks what is true,
for my lips detest wickedness.
—PROVERBS 8:6–7 (NIV)—

For there is not a word in my tongue,
but, lo, O LORD, thou knowest it altogether.
—PSALMS 139:4 (KJV)—

Let my mouth be filled with thy praise and
with thy honour all the day.
—PSALMS 71:8 (KJV)—

The mouth of a righteous man is a well of life:
but violence covereth the mouth of the wicked.
—PROVERBS 10:11 (KJV)—

The Lord GOD has given Me
the tongue of the learned,
that I should know how to speak a word
in season to him who is weary.
He awakens me morning by morning,
he awakens my ear to hear as the learned.
—ISAIAH 50:4 (NKJ)—

I said, "I will guard my ways,
lest I sin with my tongue;
I will restrain my mouth with a muzzle,
while the wicked are before me."
—PSALMS 39:1 (NKJ)—

*Like apples of gold in settings of silver is a
word spoken in right circumstances.*
—PROVERBS 25:11 (NAS)—

*Thou shalt also decree a thing, and it shall be
established unto thee and the light shall shine upon
thy ways.*
—JOB 22:28 (KJV)—

To order additional copies of this book call:

(888) 339-3782
(Toll Free; Credit Cards only)

Contact the author at:

The Pegues Group
P.O. Box 78201
Los Angeles, California 90016
(323) 293-5861
e-mail: dpegues@earthlink.net

**Also available through
Wisdom Publishing
by Deborah Smith Pegues:**

MANAGING CONFLICT GOD'S WAY

"SHOW ME THE MONEY!"